DAD AND BETH CLEAN UP

by Stephen Berry
illustrated by David Armitage

"This place is a mess," said Dad.
"We must clean it up."

"I'll help," said Beth.
"Good," said Dad. "You tidy. I'll vacuum and dust."

Dad dusted the book shelves . . .

and Beth began to put away her books.

Dad cleaned on top of the cabinet . . .

and Beth started to clean up her toys.

Dad polished the mirror . . .

and Beth began to pick up her comics.

Dad vacuumed under the table . . .

and Beth found her lost pens and pencils.

Dad dusted the chairs . . .

and Beth looked for somewhere to put her scissors and paper.

Dad stopped for a rest.

"Let's have a break," he said.

"Good idea," said Beth . . .

"Cleaning up is hard work."

16